Recorder Duets
from the Beginning

John Pitts

Duet playing brings extra pleasure to all involved, and with it an incentive to learn new notes and rhythms in order to succeed. A simultaneous development of listening skills and concentration is also required for successful ensemble playing.

Recorder Duets from the Beginning Books 1, 2 and *3* provide a wide range of repertoire to encourage duet playing by descant recorder players, both accompanied and unaccompanied. All the items are carefully graded, both in range of notes (pitches) included and in the level of difficulty. It is expected that players using Book 1 will have already reached the end of *Recorder from the Beginning Book 1*, in the author's widely popular teaching scheme.

Early pieces have matching rhythms in both parts, making it easier for the players to keep in time together. Then some independence of parts is gradually introduced, including the use of imitation and counting of rests, plus more sophisticated rhythms.

The Pupil's Books include guitar chord symbols, and the Latin American items have suggestions for use of percussion instruments. The Teacher's Books include piano accompaniments for all the duets as well as the Latin American percussion parts.

In keeping with the 'repertoire' nature of the books, only a minimum of teaching help or explanation is given. Where more help is required it is best to refer to the appropriate pages of the teaching scheme *Recorder from the Beginning*.

Order No. CH61213

Music processed by Stave Origination.
Cover photography by Patrick Harrison.
Cover design by Jon Forss.
Printed in the EU.

ISBN: 978-0-7119-5861-0

CHESTER MUSIC

part of **WiseMusic***Group*

EXCLUSIVELY DISTRIBUTED BY
HAL•LEONARD®

Visit Hal Leonard Online at
www.halleonard.com

Contact us:
Hal Leonard
7777 West Bluemound Road
Milwaukee, WI 53213
Email: info@halleonard.com

In Europe, contact:
Hal Leonard Europe Limited
42 Wigmore Street
Marylebone, London, W1U 2RY
Email: info@halleonardeurope.com

In Australia, contact:
Hal Leonard Australia Pty. Ltd.
4 Lentara Court
Cheltenham, Victoria, 3192 Australia
Email: info@halleonard.com.au

Contents

*Notes listed as 'included' do not necessarily appear often in the piece.
Some may occur only once or twice in a piece!
It is best to assess each item individually.

Way Down South

See how both recorder parts move together in this duet.
Try to play the notes exactly in time, listening carefully.

Introduction: count 4 bars

Way down South where ba - na - nas grow, A grass - hop - per stepped on an el - e - phant's toe. The el - e - phant said with tears in his eyes, 'Pick on some - bo - dy your own size.'

Les Bouffons (French)

Recorder 2 repeats the same rhythm in each bar. A repeating pattern is called an **ostinato.**

Introduction: count 2 bars

Irish Lullaby

Introduction: count 4 bars

Both recorder parts move together in this tune – except for just one bar. Then Recorder 1 has an extra note. Can you find this bar?

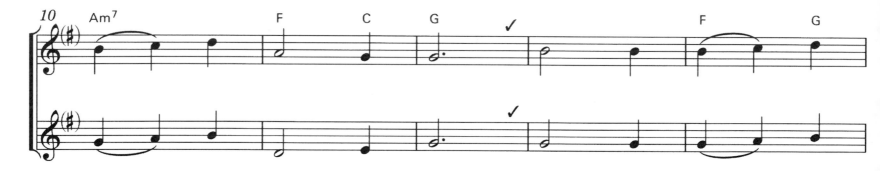

Chandos Fanfare   Pitts

You will need to listen to each other carefully in this duet and count the rests. Recorder 1 begins first, then Recorder 2 copies with some of the same music. When one part copies another we call it **imitation.**

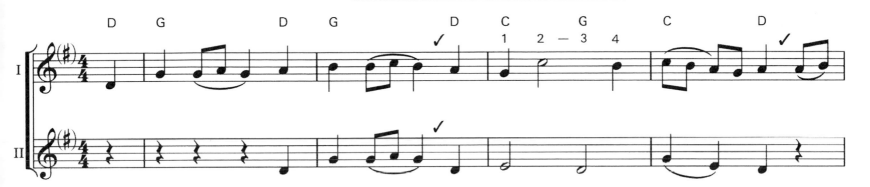

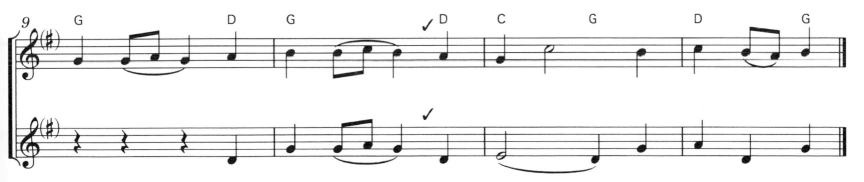

Ode To Joy   Beethoven

This tune is from Beethoven's 9th Symphony, 1824.
Take care with the tied notes at the end of line 3.

Introduction: count 2 bars

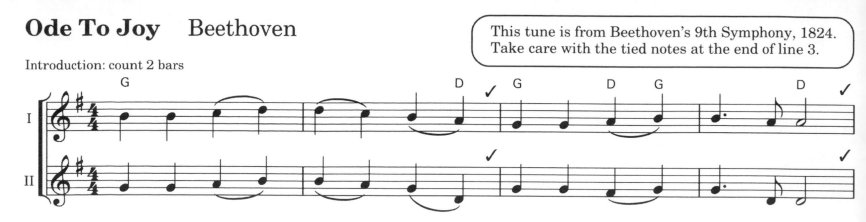

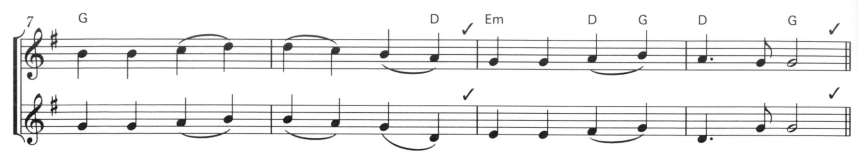

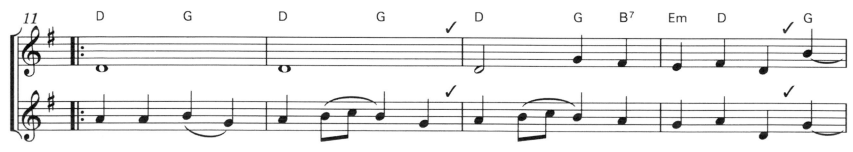

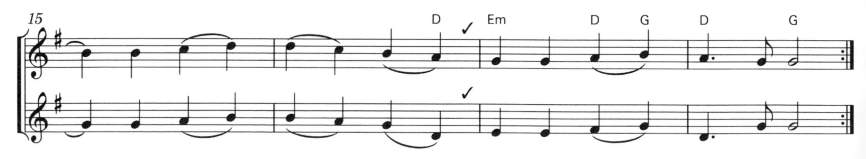

Banks of the Ohio

See how tune II echos tune I.
Listen to each other carefully as you play.

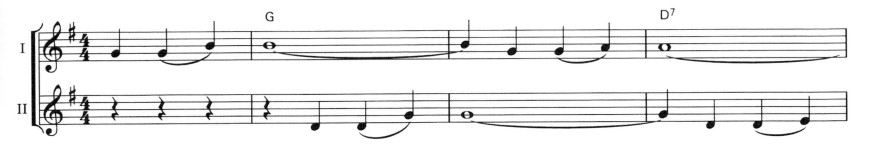

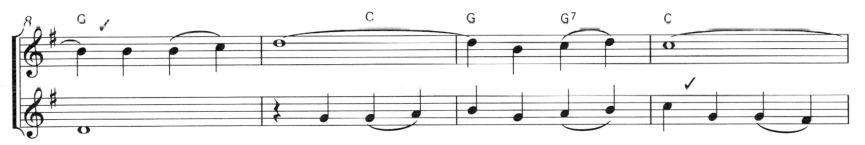

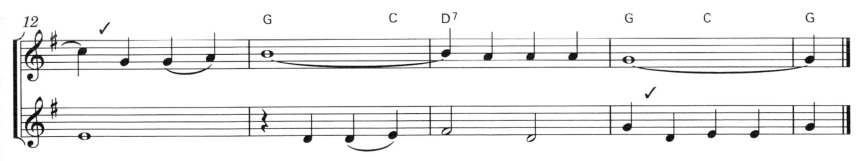

Fais Dodo   French Lullaby

Introduction: count 4 bars

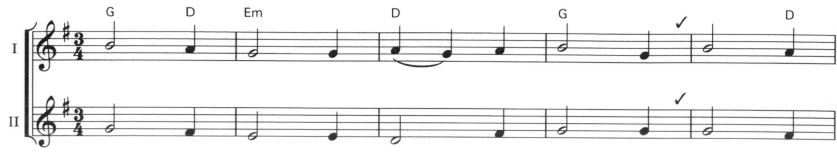

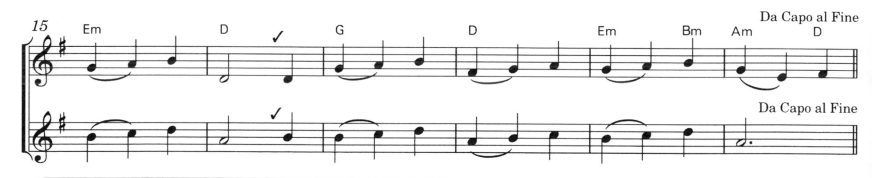

> **D.C. (Da Capo)** means go back to the beginning, and repeat
> until **Fine** (pronounced 'Feenay'). This means end.

Now All the Forests   German

The second half of Recorder 1 music (after **A**) is almost the same as the first half. Just the ending is changed. But the second half of Recorder 2 music is different from the first half, so take extra care.

Pokare Kare   Maori Song

Both tunes use exactly the same rhythm.
Take care to play in time together.

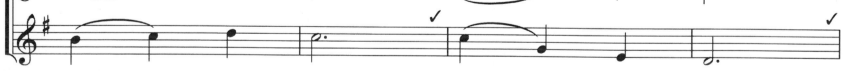

Kaluszin Mazurka Pitts

Introduction: count 4 bars (see Teacher's Book)

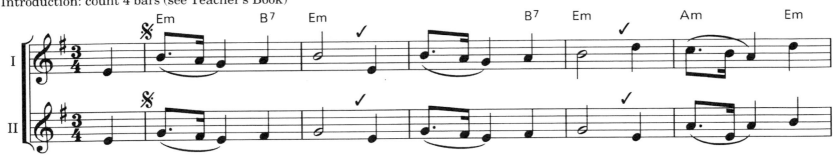

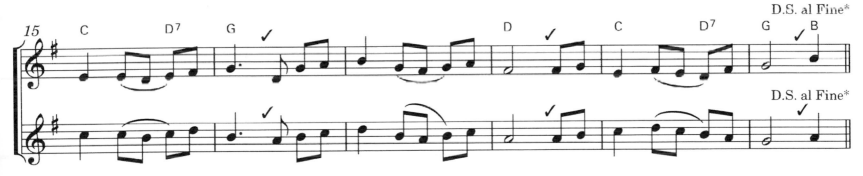

* See page 14 for explanation

The **mazurka** is a Polish national dance in triple time, often with strong accents on the second or third beat.

A mazurka by Chopin appears in Recorder Duets from the Beginning Book 2.

Tango Chacabuco Pitts

D.S. or Dal Segno means go back to the sign 𝄋
Then repeat the music until **Fine** (end).

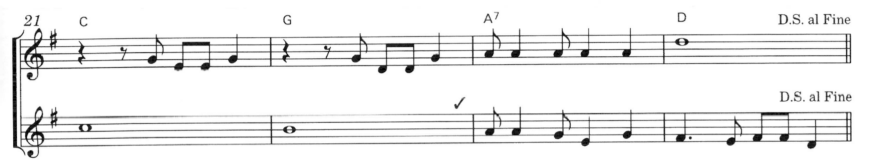

The **tango** is a Latin American dance from Argentina, with a catchy rhythm. About 1915 the tango became popular in Europe as a ballroom dance. Later it was used by many composers as an independent instrumental piece.

Ask a friend to play the first rhythm on either claves or castanets to accompany the duet.

Another friend could play the second rhythm on tambourine or jingle ring.

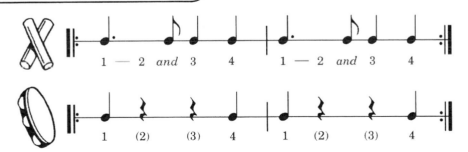

Michael, Row the Boat Ashore

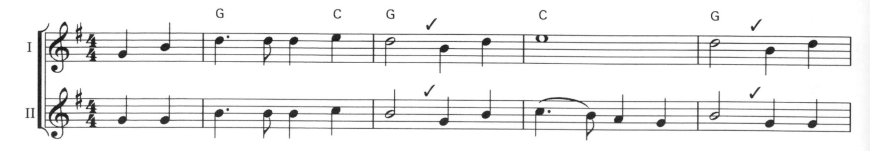

Gavotte   Handel

> Recorder 2 imitates Recorder 1 at the beginning of each line. So listen and count the rests carefully.

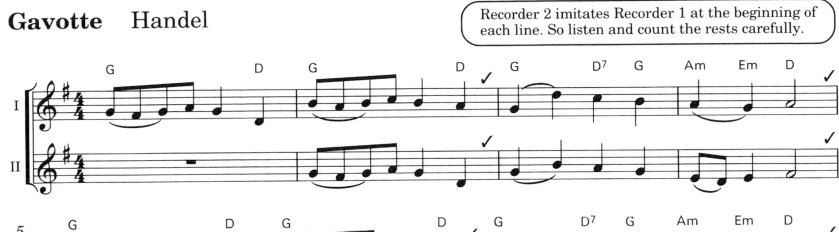

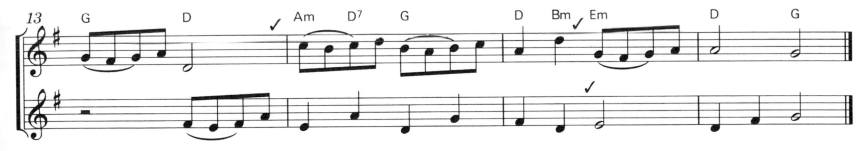

Soracaba Beguine   Pitts

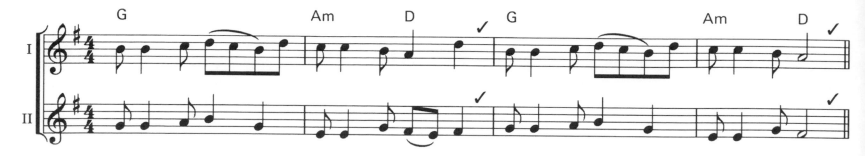

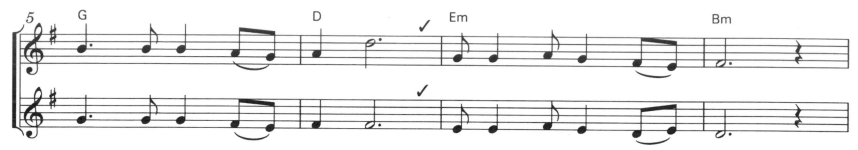

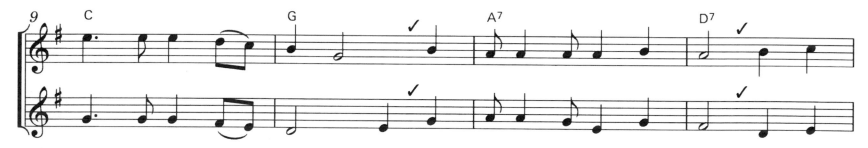

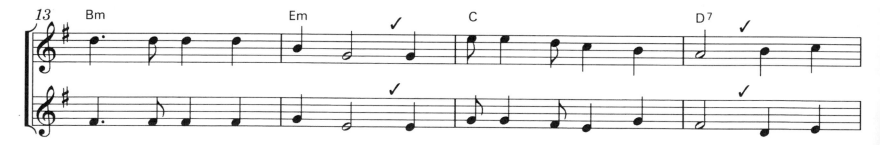

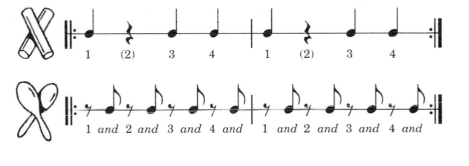

The **beguine** is a dance from South America. It combines two rhythms. Ask a friend to play the first rhythm on claves. Then a second friend can join in on maracas, playing the second rhythm at the same time.

A good idea is for player 2 to count aloud. Tap your foot for each beat (1 - 2 - 3 - 4) and play the maracas in between each time as you say '**and**'.

   1 and 2 and 3 and 4 and

Rigaudon   Chédeville

Introduction: count 4 bars (see Teacher's Book)

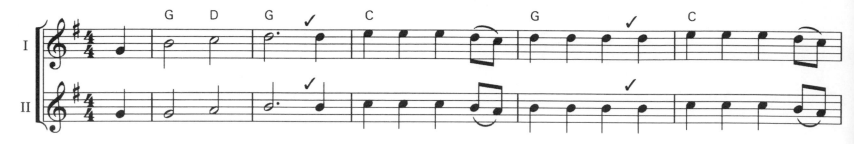

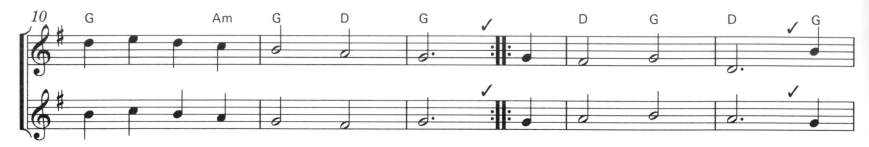

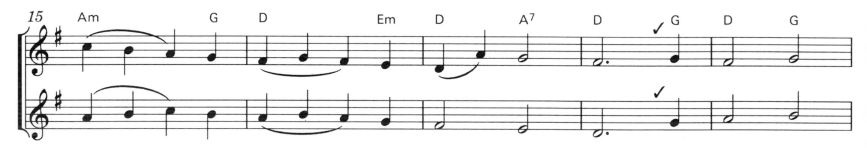

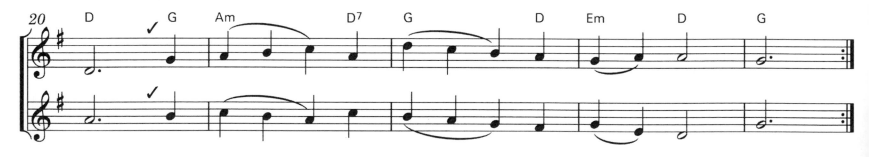

Ye Banks and Braes   Scottish

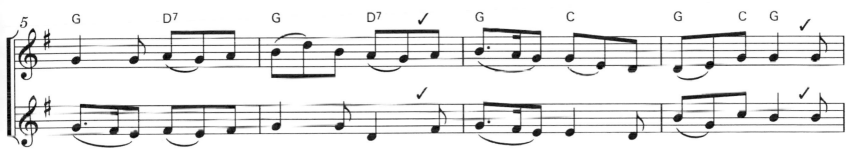

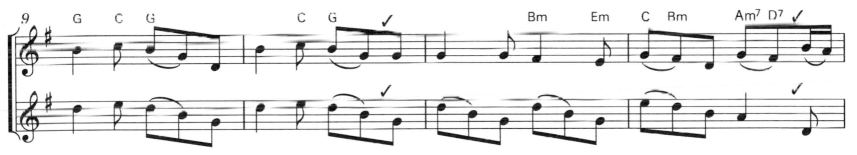

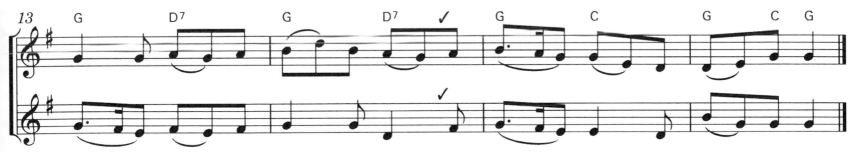

Boogie Blues   Pitts

Introduction: count 4 bars

Boogie-woogie was a special type of early piano jazz music. It first became popular in America in the 1920's, then quickly became famous throughout the world and still is today. The pieces are usually 12 bars long, with rhythmic phrases using dotted notes as in this piece. The music here also uses the traditional pattern of chords called a **12 bar blues.**

Tango La Pampa Pitts

Take care when a new phrase begins at the **end** of a line.

Introduction: count 4 bars

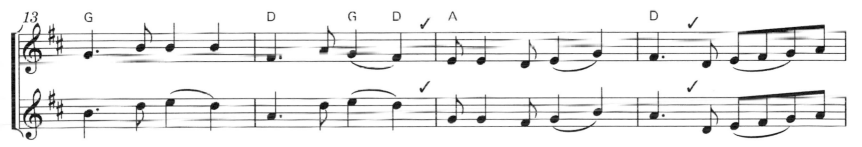

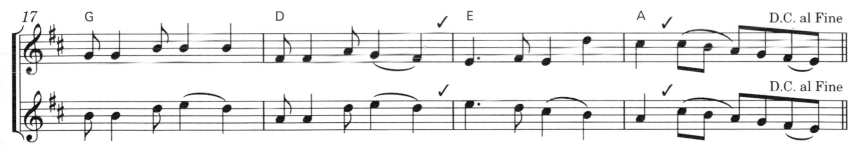

*A Tango accompaniment is shown on page 15.

The Pearly Adriatic   Yugoslavian

The note under a pause sign ⌢ should be lengthened. A total length of about double the normal value is usually right.

Introduction: count 5 bars

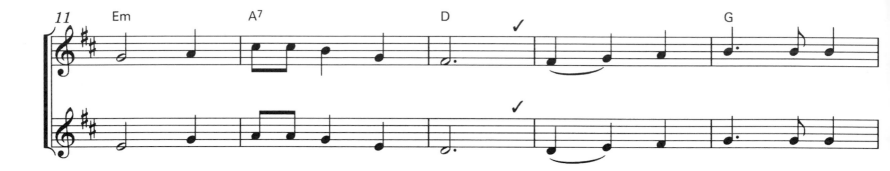

Take care at the change of time from $\frac{3}{4}$ to $\frac{2}{4}$, and then back again. The **speed** of the quarter note (crotchet) beat remains the same ($\quarternote = \quarternote$) but the change of time simply makes the $\frac{2}{4}$ section feel much faster.

Scarborough Fair

Introduction: count 5 bars

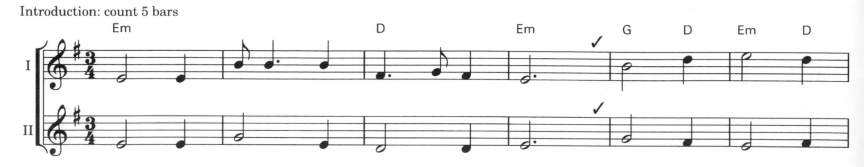

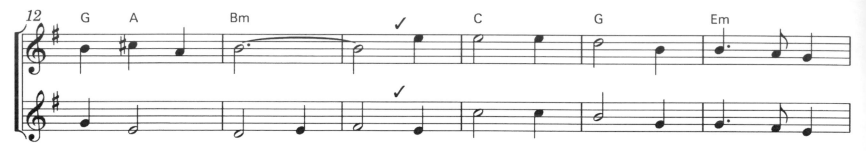

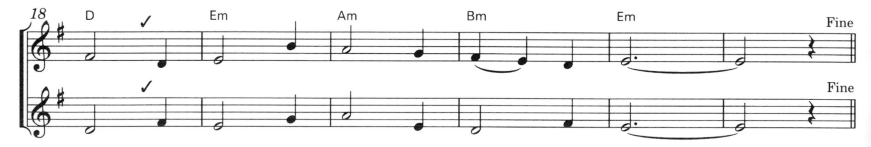

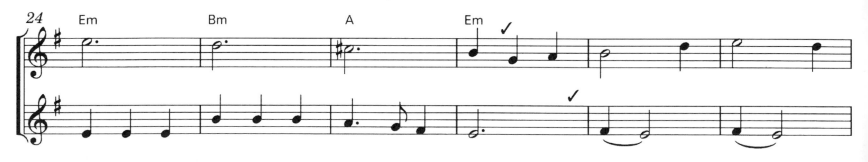

This famous English folksong dates from at least early 17th century. The tune has an unusual sound because it uses the Dorian mode, a different type of scale that was used in early times.

In this duet Recorder 1 doesn't play the tune all the time. After bar 19, each Recorder takes it in turn to play part of the tune. Recorder 2 begins. Can you find where the tune goes back to Recorder 1? Then where does the tune go back to Recorder 2 again?

Menuetto W.A. Mozart

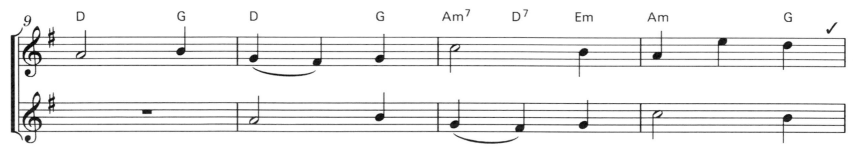

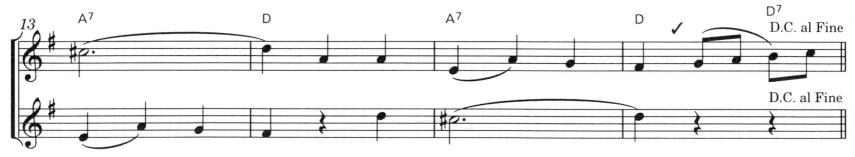

Panis Angelicus César Franck

* Piano plays this 4 bar interlude.

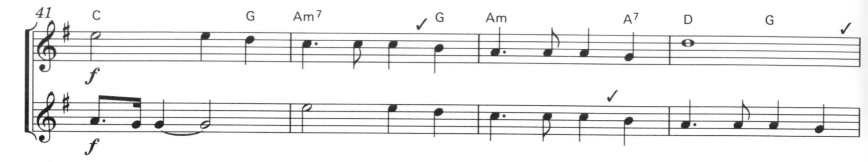

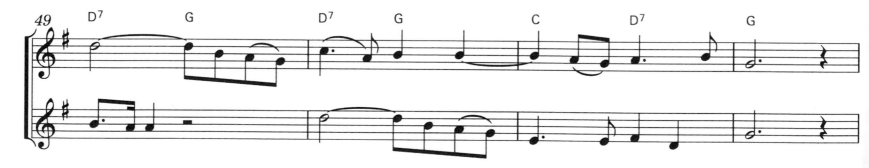

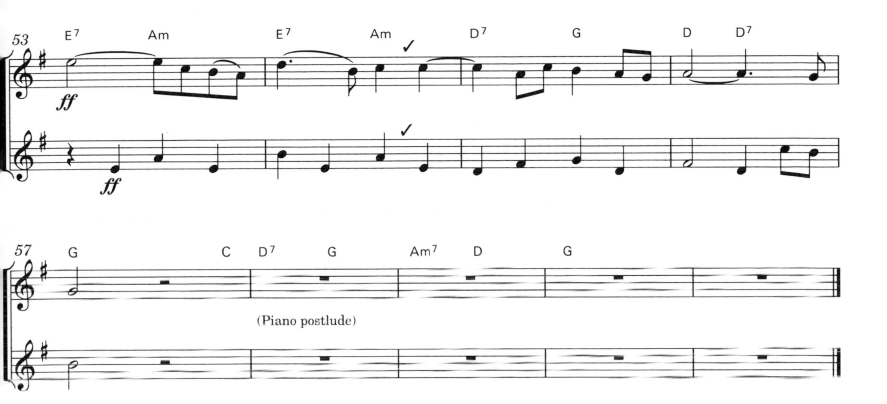

(Piano postlude)

This piece was originally a song, sometimes performed in church.

When parts I and II divide, see how both recorders use the same tune. But Recorder 2 begins one bar later, rather like an echo. When this happens we call the music a **canon.**

Fingering Chart
English (Baroque) Fingered Recorders

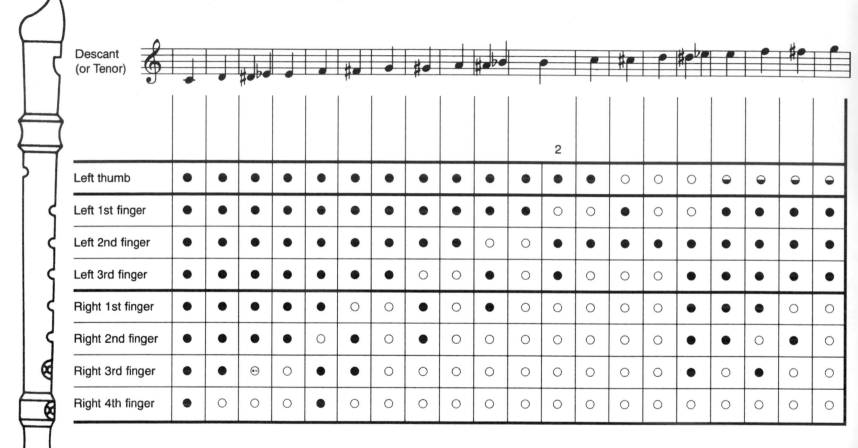

○ Open hole
● Closed hole
◐ Partly closed hole
2 Alternative fingering